Silhouettes
of
My Soul

By
Debra McLain

Silhouettes of My Soul
By
Debra McLain

2nd Edition: 2019

This Publishing is protected under Copyright Law as a "Collection". All rights for all submissions are retained by the Individual Author and or Artist. No part of this publishing may be Reproduced, Transferred in any manner without the prior **WRITTEN CONSENT** of the "Material Owner".

Publisher Information
2nd Edition: Debra Kay McLain

This Collection is protected under U.S. and International Copyright laws

Copyright © 2015: Debra McLain
Cover Design by Romano Art

ISBN: 9781709438974
Imprint: Independently published

$9.99

Dedication

Sasha and Brittany, my beautiful daughters, without you and my precious grandchildren, life would be void of all meaning. Thank you for always being here.

Preface

Silhouettes of My Soul, is like reading private love letters in the form of poetry. Silhouettes will resonate with all men and women in the pursuit of love and happiness. Striving for personal growth, Debra writes of relationships, nature, and the universe.

Table of Contents

Table of Contents ... continued

Table of Contents ... continued

Epilogue

Silhouettes
of
My Soul

By
Debra McLain

Alone

The haunting sounds of yesterday,
always present, lurking in the dark corners.
Secluded, she tries to hide from the whispers.
Sad memories invade her sacred space...
Wrapped in solitary confinement,
she attempts to disappear.

Angels Whisper

When my soul is tired, and needs to rest,
I ask for guidance and strength to go on.
Angels whisper and request that I listen,
for they will sing, when I play their song.
There is a melody within, only I can hear,
a rhythm so soothing, it brings forth the light.
Sometimes, I forget, about the music inside,
it hides under the scars, that never heal right.
My wounds are my demons, they like to play,
invading my thoughts, telling me vicious lies.
I cast them aside, order them to go away...
Ready to play a masterpiece, the angels sigh.

Art of Nature

The sun hides, blue skies turns gray,
air weighs me down, can hardly breathe.
I miss your touch, sweet whispers of love,
only sleepless nights, and exhausted days.
Thunderstorms threaten, lightning strikes,
my soul is weary, these afflictions are real.
Wide-open spaces, keep us so far apart,
our love is strong, and for that, I will fight.
Leaves shall fall, when summer parts,
colors, will cast their light on my soul.
As nights get longer, and each day fades,
the heart finds strength, in nature's art.

Autumn Breeze

Summer slowly dies, Autumn comes alive,
tints of brownish gold, striking hues of red.
Heavy sighs, salty tears, behind lidded eyes,
a solemn song rustles through the leaves.
Your body decayed, before I said goodbye,
one week in September, brings me grief.
I long for an Autumn, when you were alive,
not like a faded leaf, blowing in the breeze.

Born Free

She is a tiger, who adores an untamed lion,
tempestuous moments, make him ROAR.
No chain shall hinder his hunger for freedom,
loose in the wild, he comes home for more.
Smokin' and drinkin', tokin' and rebellin',
unbridled, on the prowl for that next high.
Conformity pains him, he was born to roam,
some don't understand his reasons why.
His feline is near, embracing his power,
a master of his domain and carnal needs.
Ferocious desires for an unrestrained life,
when trapped in a cage, his soul bleeds.

Bull's Eye

oh baby
I love the way
you flirt and tease
a big ole' bull's eye
splashed across
your manly chest
it screams at me...
"hit me please!"
am I hopeless
or just insane
for thinking
your wild heart
may be tamed?
willing to play
loves silly game
I cross my heart
hope to die
close one eye
one, two, three, aim
BULLS EYE!
life is never
gonna be the same

Burning Love

He ignites my flame,
with one little glance.
A roaring fire, untamed,
my soul, a flaming dance.

Together, our bodies burn,
a combustion of heat & light.
For him, my body yearns,
embers, smoldering in the night.

Calm During the Storm

A storm brews, beyond the horizon, lightning
collides with sunshine, intermittent booms.
Negative energy, thrashes about violently
in one's own mind, a disturbance of balance.
It is natural, to feel alone, as thunder crashes
in the atmosphere, peace whispers, barely heard.
Feel me, hold my hand across the distance,
know you are not alone, as the commotion roars.

Confliction

Whispers echo in my mind, altercations
between extreme sorrow and well-being.
Desolation or contentment, up, down
continuous changes, rarely foreseeing.
Days of depression, a bleak atmosphere,
not understanding, when there is no hope.
Light, on the horizon, glimmers of sanity,
smiles replace tears, another day I cope.

Contentment

A gentle brook of crystal water,
through the tainted mind flows.
Her image resembles peace and joy,
sparkling diamonds all aglow.
A tiny stream of contentment
roars behind tear stained eyes.
The imagination is a precious gift,
it comforts, when the heart cries.

Desert Rose

she no longer hurts
her heart is not there
no more searching
for sustainment
in secluded places
a desert rose
seeking protection
from the scorching sun
abandoned and hungry
her heart always burning
she forgot her worth
when petals were wilting
stems, on the brink of decay
mirages brought yearning
for anything to ease the thirst
just when she thought
the desert was dry
her roots dug deep
thorns began kneeling
God's pure love
granted her soul
a rain filled day
of nourishing healing

Destination Unknown

In this journey of life
I sometimes lose direction
goals and expectations
not surveyed on the map.

The road before me crumbles
into an abyss of despair
no longer do I understand
why, when or where.

Free falling in the dark
grasping for the edge
life and promise evade me
doubts are found instead.

A small flicker of light
in the corners of my mind
become a shining beacon
sadness bursts into flames.

Fear cannot restrain me
my fire burns bright
love... takes over the wheel
no longer do I drive.

Diamond in the Sand

I will hold
  your heart
ever so gently
  like a diamond
among the sand
  a treasure
not to take
  for granted
I know the value
  in my hands

Explosion

every moment with him
is a nuclear distraction
an explosive release
of energetic reactions

my senses detonate
emotions implode
huge balls of fire
through my veins flow

Feel Me

his hand, touches the small of my back
while we stand in line
a simple gesture, lets me know I am his
as he gently nudges me forward

his finger, sweeps the curl out of my eye
before we kiss
he loves my wild hair, says its sexy
yet he wants no distraction, from my lips

his forehead, leans into mine
chakra to chakra
he reads my every thought
through the tremors of my vibration

his eyes, gaze into mine
they shoot arrows of truth
into my soul, so deep
it can be felt behind closed lids

he is out there, he knows not
who I am, by my voice
only that I am here
waiting for him to find me

Floating

I reach for the light in my imagination,
a life raft, among a sea of despair.
Darkness threatens to drown me,
days filled, with unanswered prayers.

The lantern shines brightly, it gives me hope,
as I grasp for the strength to swim.
Moments filled with smiles and love,
keep me afloat, while the moon is dim.

Flying

Oh, so high, I fly,
  feather floating
    soft, tame breeze.

Over the mountains,
  across the sea
    light, gentle, free.

Drifting silently,
  poetic whispers
    of redwood trees.

No fear, no worry,
  happy as can be
    gliding, with ease.

Forever Yours

our lips met in
sweet anticipation
all of our secrets
were exposed

a solitary kiss
tingling sensations
truth was tasted
my heart said, "I know"

your mind caressed
my broken soul
gentle hands
ran through my hair

you whispered
that you love me
I will be yours
forever, if you dare

Forgotten Children

Their voices still echo in the halls,
"Come, little ones, it is time for a meal!"
Boys, rush to put away their basketballs,
girls, stop playing tag, no more squeals.

Too many children, not enough homes,
they waited, with no choice, but to stay.
Some were adopted, others, left to roam,
hoping for parents, each and every day.

Lost in the system, time passed them by,
growing up in an orphanage, no one to love.
No kisses for booboos, or when they cried,
love is all they wanted, what they dreamed of.

Sadness lingers, it is imprinted in rooms,
haunting the home, with whispers and tears.
It sits on a hill, in grandeur and gloom,
ghostly children still play, after all of these years.

Galaxy

the moon
is nothing
compared
to the stars
in your soul
let me write
poetry
on your heart
so the galaxy
shines out
of your eyes

Goddess of Love

Deep in the forest, where no human dwells,
lives the Goddess of Love, or so legend tells.
An enchanting beauty, with flaming red hair,
a lyrical voice that floats through the air.
A mythical being, she has never been seen,
her life is a fable, so magically serene.
Affection is chanted, heard by the heart,
everlasting devotion, an immortal art.

Healing Nature

What happened to the wind,
that made it turn against the rain?
No longer do they coincide,
one claims to be right, the other wrong,
one justifies anger, the other is in pain.
Mother Earth covers her sorrowful eyes,
as she wishes to be deaf and blind.
A gentle sigh as she weeps in vain,
not happy her children are being unkind.
Not even the sun comes out to play,
the moon goes dark, and stars pay no mind.
Not happy in a world with fear and disdain,
the universe intervenes and speaks her truth,
compassion for another, is what she seeks.
With a promise of love and eternal devotion,
Mother Earth extends her loving arms,
she whispers of peace to heal and soothe.

Heart Afflictions

Hush now, my beating heart,
tranquility may be found in the stillness.
Acknowledge your suffering,
trust, your afflictions are temporary.

Vulnerability entices you to self-destruct,
promises... will lure you into the dark spaces.
Remember, your fire burns like a thousand suns,
a strength so intense, the pain, erupts in flames.

Cherish the memories, they are eternally yours.
No experience goes without lessons.
The challenge is to remain strong,
for you have the power to be invincible.

Heart on Fire

a little spark
set afire by
his poetic pen

passions flare
sizzling words
have me yearning

intensity grows
immortal ink flows
pages keep turning

my tender heart
smolders slowly
from the burning

He Loves Me...

My heart beats, for the one I adore,
palpitations, from his words and more.
He is a poet, the inspiration, for my writes,
longing for him, lasts throughout the night.
Sleep deprived, needing of affection,
I busy my mind, changing directions.
No holding my breath, for things to change,
he stays at a distance, out of my range.

Home

There she is, on a humid summer day,
a stranger in an eerie place, nobody sees.
Whispers of grief, drift through the air,
ancient trees sigh, longing for a breeze.
She does not belong, this is not her home,
crickets sing a sad song, birds chime in.
Rugged in appearance, with loving eyes,
he appears before her, deep pain within.
Broken, beaten down from a great loss,
she pulls him in, anticipating his lips.
A yearning is felt, within his embrace,
she suddenly knows, Home is where he is.

I Know Prince Charming

Look at you, sitting on your white horse,
so handsome, suave, and debonair.
Armor... spit-shined, silver, and bright,
maidens kneel down, with long flowing hair.
A knight of honor, compassion, and hope,
rescuing women there and here.
Uninhibited, and free, to do as you wish,
your words are smooth, a voice sincere.
Sexy eyes, and touch so smooth,
you speak poetry, it makes them shiver.
Prince Charming is not a myth, oh, no he's not,
you ride in swiftly, the ever-gallant giver.
Swooning dames, who offer their love,
kissing your feet, to show appreciation.
Every woman wants a chivalrous man,
thousands like you, would change civilization.

Intuitive Whispers

His words, splash across the canvas,
an artist of eloquent expression.
Mentally calling upon creative geniuses,
emotions are imprinted on his soul.
Sensitive to the words of Poe,
intuition maneuvers his pen.
Breathing in the love of art,
he exhales today's masterpiece.

Irish Rose

Sentiments of his adoration, linger,
after he leaves the room, yet, she cries.
She holds on to last night's memories,
never knowing, if they are goodbye.
Is her love enough, to be his forever?
No longer a thorn, her petals came alive,
an Irish Rose, hoping their love will survive.

It's Complicated

Thoughts of him cause a sensory explosion,
as his energy drifts across the distance.
My brain detonates, leaving a vacant space,
the heart attempts to blocks its existence.

Follow my head, or follow my heart?
There are complications that arise.
With the brain, I know the consequences,
the heart tells me, our love will never die.

I Will Remember

I stand on your grave weeping alone,
tears fall on your name, carved in stone.
You went to battle on a ghastly ride,
never to return to a brokenhearted bride.

Shadows danced across the distant plain,
darkness prevailed, my brave man slain.
I heard you call in the dead of night,
my name on your lips, as you seen the light.

Rest now, my darling, sleep in peace,
our love is eternal, it shall never cease.
Reunited, we will be, in another life,
vows will be remembered, as man and wife.

Living Art

The blank paper waits,
for the artist,
to bring forth life.
Perhaps, she will paint her mood,
black, with a dash of complexities.
Or what she longs for,
vibrant orange, passion.
The many colors of life,
ever changing.
A splash of yellow,
for the coward who hurt her.
Or, a lovely shade of red,
for her still beating heart.
The paper is bare,
waiting for her hands,
to create a masterpiece.

Magic Moments

moonbeam's of silver
cast a poetic spell
two lovers, a new start
she dances only for him
this man has her heart
swaying to the music
taunting with her eyes
enchanted moments
anticipated sighs
honeysuckle and rose
drift through the air
he leans down for a kiss
whispering promises
gently touching her hair
magic moments in time
the earth stops spinning
nothing compares
to loves great beginning

Magic Pen

Letters flow through his pen,
conjuring magic, to behold.
Words of enchantment,
cast a spell upon my soul.
Fairy dust pours from his ink well,
moments, immortalized in time.
True life stories bewitch me,
a stimulation to my mind.

Midnight Moon

Moonbeams illuminate
two souls, embracing the wind
mind and body entwined
infinite celestial blessings
from stars and universe aligned.

Provocative glances
wild passions heightened
heat vapors rise like a balloon
a veil of love creates the clouds
surrounding a midnight moon.

New Directions

Life plays misleading games,
flamboyant skies masquerade,
temporal illusions of grandeur.
A masterpiece of misconception,
it passes us by, the scarlet fades,
as winds change in a new direction.

Numb

Loved ones die unexpectedly.
A warm heart turns cold.
Grief devours our living soul.
"I am fine", a hopeful lie.
Attempts to be whole,
words are expressed,
from lips that bleed.
Tears fall in torrents,
salt stains on sheets.
That horrid ache is felt,
down to our very core.
An intensity so strong,
it hurts to breathe.
With a heavy heart,
veins turn to stone.
They do not understand...
We do not want company,
yet, it is what we need.
Often told to move on,
"they are in a better place".
Useless words,
when you feel the thorn.
There is no secret garden
of pretty red roses,
in the heart that hardens.
Prayers for comfort,
soon turns to begging,
"God, please heal this pain",

Cont....

Silhouettes of My Soul

eventually wishing
you'd never been born.
We have to work,
got to pay the bills.
Time passes slowly,
world keeps spinning.
Doctors prescribe pills,
anything to numb the brain.
It gets better for a while.
Then one day,
another loved one dies.
No more living in denial,
life passes us by,
There are more tears to cry,
when we finally realize,
no one is here to stay.

Only You

There is nothing more spectacular than looking into your
eyes, and seeing pure love.
The entire galaxy could land at my feet, asking for
attention. I would still see, only you.

Peace

My skin feels the sun, I inhale the hot rays,
heat drifts through the air, enveloping me.
I am grateful for the water that gently flows,
trees that sing wistfully, in a calming breeze.
Nature brings joy to my restless heart,
every day is a blessing, I know to be true.
Yet, each day is the same, he is not here,
a promise has been made, to never let go.
With empty arms, I stand alone in my tears,
an embrace is needed, only he can provide.
My aching heart is open, the love pours in,
peace has renewed my lone beating heart.
When I am sad and need another escape,
I sit on my porch and close my eyes.
He is always with me, his hand is in mine,
my imagination soars, like a bird in the sky.
I can smell pine trees, hear the waterfalls,
everything I wish for, is in my mind's eye.

Perception

Wildflowers are scattered, growing free,
delicate, yet strong, braving the elements.
One little flower, unrestrained, exquisite,
or a weed, depending on one's perception.
A field of flora, varied colors and types,
short or tall, a natural will to survive.
Differences admired, gardens are created,
standing together, beautifully united.

Perfect in the Sky

he calls me baby
from the phone line
my heart skips
head floats
above the clouds
livin' on cloud nine
I never want
to come down
from this eternal high
I choose to live
where I am happy
life is perfect
in the sky

Poetic Rebel

My mind ponders in adoration, complete
fascination, over such a creative genius...
An articulate sculptor of the written word.

Liquid verses, heat flows, molten silver,
artistic prose, molded to perfection...
Likened to a statue, high upon a pedestal.

Resistant to strict Southern tradition,
his poetic passion is only heightened...
As society places him in a structured box.

Undeniably rebellious by nature, authority
brings forth passionate scribes, whispers...
From the pen of a gentlemanly renegade.

Positive Vibrations

Every thought is a vibration,
energy waves of color
sent out into the universe.

Every word spoken,
reshapes the frequency
around others and ourselves.

Let us be love,
'good vibes' shift the matrix
that will change our world.

Regrets

Every morning brings awareness,
as my regrets are brought to light.
Too many words were said in anger,
I no longer have the strength to fight.
In my heart, it does not matter,
if you were wrong, or I was right.
Forgiveness can be a challenge,
when fear creates so many doubts.
However, love, overcomes all obstacles,
I know now, what I cannot live without.
With you by my side, my life is complete,
together, any and everything is possible.

Reminiscence

Birds chirp in the old oak tree,
magnolia blossoms dancing free.
She writes her sweetheart,
on rose-colored stationery.
Memories of her loving arms,
keepsakes keep his heart from harm.
She tells him of her wishful dreams,
inscribed with all her subtle charm.
Moonlight glows inside the den,
adjacent to her desk and pen.
Stars shine bright, to wish upon,
desire keeps him close within.
Waxed and sealed, a gentle kiss,
sent with care, her words of bliss.
In times when he feels all alone,
he will read her words and reminisce.

Sad Moon

Morning dew, cradles the moon,
soothing her troubles and fears.
Comforting is the warm embrace,
as she blends her vapors with tears.
Twinkling stars shine bright with love,
promising her troubles will cease.
If only she believes, staying true to self,
the universe shall bring her peace.

Skies of Fire

Star-lit waters glisten
under a sunset of gold.
Seagulls stop and listen
to whispers of the cold.
Ocean salted perfume
wafts gently in the air.
Mother earths womb
tells me that she cares.
Rolling waves leap higher
a desire to be free.
Painted skies of fire
before my eyes to see.

Stardust

Sometimes
in brief moments
of clarity
cosmic encounters
enlighten the
consciousness.

A transparent bubble
of protection
explodes
every cell of reality
releases an
atomic energy.

Tiny fragments
of the soul
float silently upward
into galaxies unknown
evaporating
into stardust.

Star Gazing

nothing is
more perfect
than this night
the universe itself
does not match
the stars I see
in your eyes
your magnetism
draws me in
our energy
so connected
we create
a new constellation

Summer of Love and Sorrow

Jeweled skies of ruby and pearl,
lustrous waves, crash against the shore.
You stand before me, a treasure I cherish,
my artistic lover, such brilliance, I adore.
Stagnant tides of grief and sorrow,
have brought forth a summer of pain.
Twilight brings hope for tomorrow,
your faith, our love, is not in vain.
Dark blue diamonds of the sea,
torrential tides with gems, in sync.
Together, we shall face all storms,
turbulence blends our love and ink.

Surrender

The door has opened,
there is no hesitation
as I step into the abyss.
Free falling in the darkness,
the euphoric feeling of relief
replenishes my weary soul.
Sweet surrender,
grasp my lungs of despair
lead me into nirvana.

Take Your Time

sunbeams
weaved between
curves and lace

delicate
illumination
imagination soars

femininity
scorching hot
intertwined

unwrap
my gift of love
take your time

The End

An endearing glance,
caught in the camera lens.
A smile so immense,
it lights up a dark room.
Words slide off the tongue,
soothing, sweet as honey.
A hug so secure,
heartbeats, become one.
Pretending is so easy,
an award winning performance.
She steals the show, takes a bow,
and keeps on living until the curtain falls.

The Hard Working Man

He dusts off his weary bones,
ignoring the aches of exhaustion.
Another twelve hours of existing,
on autopilot with every motion.

A piercing pain in his heart,
dismissed after an insufficient nap.
Fatigue is just a way of life,
stumbling blindly into deaths trap.

Wanting to make a difference,
perfection at his craft, brings pride.
Working his fingers to the bone,
a burned out brain, sleep is denied.

A hard working man, living life,
every day, like the one before.
Choices are made, without a thought,
dying inside, he heads out the door.

Till The End of Time

Your arms may be empty, but never your heart.
For there I reside, waiting, for our life to start.
You may cuddle the ink, it is good for your soul.
Yet, snuggling with me, will never grow old.
Let the magic flow, from your masterful pen.
Reading your words, gives me chills deep within.
We share the same moon, and beautiful stars.
Nowhere in the galaxy, is there a love like ours.
Love is not a game two lovers should play.
When love is for real, the heart always knows.
The fire is burning, can you not hear my flames?
My heart is in yearning, it is yours to claim.
Distance does not matter, when love is predestined.
I am yours, you are mine, of that I am certain.
Nights without you here, do appear to be longer.
With patience, my darling, our love will grow stronger.
Hush now and listen, I whisper only the truth.
I shall love you till the end of time, let my words soothe.
For in you, I have found my beginning and end.
Till death do us part, two poets, who share a poetic pen.

Torrential Heart

turbulence
  disrupts the peace
in her soul
  feelings
vigorously agitate
  as passion swells
torrents of emotions
  crash against the shores
of love
  does she dare?
is there such a man?
  who can turn
her torrential heart
  into a peaceful stream?
or
  will happiness
flow rapidly
  through his heart
creating a tsunami
  of destruction?

Umbrella

my heart skipped a beat
you were standing there
red umbrella, a smile
full of promises and hope
I want this baby
walks in the rain
you and me
hand in hand
it is where I want to be
I am giving it all I've got
my heart, on a sleeve
whenever you have doubts
look into my eyes and see
your life is not
complete, without me
let me be your umbrella
when life rains
on your parade
I will shield you with love
always, forever, today

United We Stand

There she flies, in all her glory,
honoring the brave and fallen.
Colors, so vibrant, tell her story,
of 'One Nation Under God'.

Red stands out, fearless courage,
integrity of men and women, sacrifice.
Devotion to the United States of America,
patriotic until their very last breath.

White, equality, fairness for all,
innocence from hatred, non-judgment.
A non-color, yet fiercely holding hands,
with the red and blue, unconditionally.

Blue, loyalty, allegiance to America,
perseverance against injustice.
Land of the free, faith in mankind,
color of Heaven, hope for humanity.

Life in America, often taken for granted,
the ability to speak without repercussions.
A country known for religious freedom,
determination, the sanctity of Home.

In the words of Abraham Lincoln,
"A government of the people,

.

Cont....

by the people, for the people".
Our flag represents ALL people

A sacred emblem of our country,
she is a symbol of our birthright.
Our heritage runs through our veins,
purchased with blood and sorrow.

She flies high, a silhouette, among
the blue sky, Old Glory, shall never die.
Desecrated, burned, stomped on, in anger,
her significance shall remain, for eternity.

Unmasked

there is pain hidden
behind the deceptive smile
a mask, made of pretense
conceals the disappointments
promises were broken
contentment fades away

she wonders what would happen
if the cloak were absent
all pretense abandoned
yesterday's wounds
revealing the imperfections
she has obscured from the light

Weeping Willow

Your magnificence astonishes me.
Oh, the strength you show,
through the droughts of yesterday,
the heat of a thousand suns.
Wind... threatening to tear your limbs.
Nature attempted to break you,
yet, only made you stronger.
Your roots, firmly planted,
dig deeper into Mother Earth.

Whirl Wind

Caught in the path of a summer storm,
winds howl in anger, no shelter is found.
Lightning screams, thunder clouds form,
overwhelmed, trying to stand her ground.
A tornado of intention, emotional twister,
no one else hears the cyclone of sounds.
Even the strongest heart will shatter,
when tossed about, without a care.
Words are like whirlwinds, they matter,
a destructive force, too much to bear.

Epilogue

Debra McLain

About the Author

Debra McLain resides in California. '*Silhouettes of My Soul*' follows her first book of poetry, '*To Conquer or Die Trying*'. From depression to healing, her words will touch you. She is mother to two daughters and three granddaughters. She works in agriculture, although her passion is in writing.